Fade, Vision Bright

Poem anonymous

NORMAN DELLO JOIO

Norman Dello Joio

Three Songs of Adieu

for High Voice and Piano

After Love
Fade, Vision Bright
Farewell

EXCLUSIVELY DISTRIBUTED BY

7777 W. BLUEMOUND RD. P.O. BOX 13819 MILWAUKEE, WI 53213

www.ebmarks.com
www.halleonard.com

After Love

Poem by Arthur Symons

NORMAN DELLO JOIO

clasping hands can pray thee;   Fare-well, de-light!

I ___ have no more   to   say   to thee. ____   The

gold   was gold   the lit-tle while   it   last-ed,   the

dream was true,   al-though its joy   be blast-ed. ____

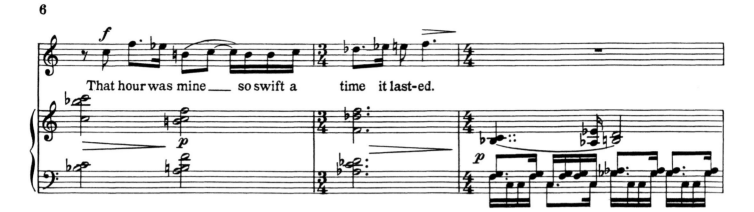

That hour was mine ___ so swift a   time   it last-ed.

Fade,   vi-sion   bright!

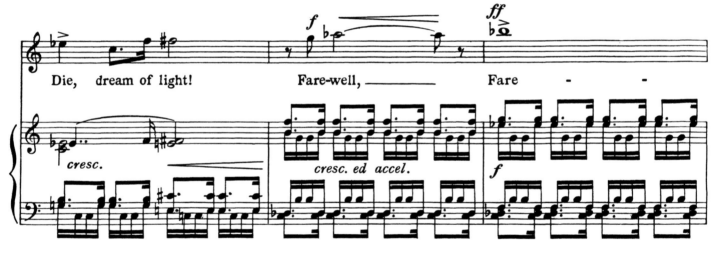

Die,   dream of light!   Fare-well, _____   Fare - -

-well. _____

Farewell

Poem by John Addington Symonds

NORMAN DELLO JOIO

night and gloom _____ I can take; _____ I do not grudge thy splend-our; _____

Bid souls of eag-er men a-wake; Be kind and bright and tend-er.

Give day to oth-er worlds; for me _____ it must suf-fice to dream of thee. _____

Fare - well, fare - well. _____

U.S. $7.95

ISBN 978-1-4803-3027-6

HL00117061

AUGUSTA READ THOMAS

DREAM CATCHER

FOR SOLO VIOLA

REVISED EDITION

G. SCHIRMER, *Inc.*

DISTRIBUTED BY

HAL•LEONARD®

Dedicated with admiration and gratitude to Carol Rodland

DREAM CATCHER

(for Solo Viola)

(solo violin version is also available)

Augusta Read Thomas
(2008)

*Bowings are only suggestions and do not have to be used.

**Grace notes have good duration and should not be rushed or slid through.

***Move from single-stops to double-stops (or vice versa) with extreme grace and elegance – never choppy.

2021 Version